One-Minute Math Developmental Drill

Grades 1-2

Table of Contents

Author: Theresa Warnick

Frank Schaffer Publications®

Send all inquiries to:
Frank Schaffer Publications
3195 Wilson Drive NW
Grand Rapids, Michigan 49534

ISBN 0-7647-0393-5

11 12 13 MAZ 09 08 07

DIRECTIONS FOR USE

Setting up the Program

Reproduce enough copies of the tests for the class. You may wish to separate the tests by fact into file folders and organize the folders in a storage box. This provides handy access to the tests and a quick view of the pages which need to be replenished.

Using a manila file folder for each student offers easy organization and provides a simple method of distributing the daily tests.

Using the Flash Cards

A set of flash cards is required for each student. These serve as additional facilitators in learning and retaining basic math facts.

When beginning the program, give each student only those facts he or she has mastered on the progress chart and the first unchecked fact. This card will correspond to the test the student will be taking. Each time another fact is mastered, give the student the card for the next fact. When starting at Zero Rule, the student should be given all the zero flash cards. You may wish to present this rule as: any number minus zero gives that number. When he or she progresses to the One Rule, the student is given all the minus one flash cards. The One Rule may be presented as: any number minus one gives the next smaller number. After this point the student will receive one flash card at a time. Unmastered flash cards may be left in the student's folder for easy access.

Encourage the use of the flash cards at home as well as at school. Depending on the number of cards being reviewed, you may wish to spend five to fifteen minutes a day on flash card practice.

Using the Bulletin Boards

The "Race for the Facts" bulletin board theme can be used to highlight the particular fact on which each student is working. Using the reproducible art found on page vi, write the math facts on the flags and write the students' names on the cars. Group their names around the particular fact on which they are working; when a fact is mastered, move that student's name card to the next fact flag.

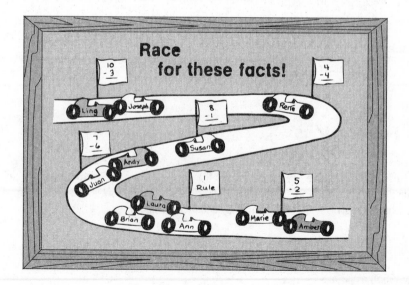

Using the Progress Charts

The progress chart shows the subtraction facts and indicates the scope and sequence of Level A (minuends zero to ten). By checking off each fact a student masters, you can record each student's progress. Each student may track his or her own progress by coloring a copy of the personal progress chart found in the reproducible pages.

The Letter to Parents

The letter provided will help make parents aware of the objectives, components and methods of the One-Minute Math Developmental Drill series.

Awards and Certificate of Achievement

When a student completes a designated number of facts, you may wish to present him or her with an award found in the reproducible pages. The certificate may be used when all of the facts in the series are mastered.

Using the Manipulative Mats

It is important that students develop a good understanding of numbers. The following activities will help students create relations for numbers and will help strengthen their number sense.

Have the students work with a variety of materials on the manipulative mats (page vii). These mats may be laminated for extended use.

1. The mat is divided into two parts. The left side contains a large X and the right side is blank. Select a number from zero to ten and have the students place that number of counters on the right side of their mats. Next, ask the students to divide their counters into two parts by moving some or all of their counters to the X'd side of their mats. Each student should verbalize the subtraction sentence he or she is demonstrating. For example, if five is the number selected, each subtraction sentence will begin with that number. If the student moves two counters to the X'd side of the mat, the sentence will be, "Five minus two equals three." Allow the students adequate practice in manipulating the counters into sets showing all possible sets for a given minuend.

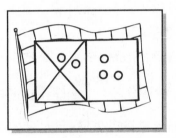

2. Students should continue working with their manipulative mats and counters. On copies of activity page viii, have the student draw the number of counters selected and cross out the number he or she is subtracting as demonstrated on the mat. Finally, the student should write the corresponding subtraction sentence.

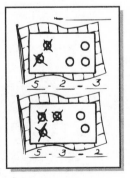

3. Have the students work with partners. Select a minuend from zero to ten and ask the students to place that number of counters on the right side of their mats. One student should divide the counters by moving some or all to the X'd side of the mat and then cover the remaining counters. For example, if five is the minuend selected and the student moves three counters to the X'd side, his or her partner must answer the question, "If three is taken from five, what number is left?" Continue this activity with all minuends of ten or less.

Using the Timed Tests

Level A Subtraction teaches minuends zero to ten. Each sheet contains 30 problems. There is a pretest and posttest for placement and evaluation. The particular fact the student is learning appears 40% of the time (twelve problems) on each test. The last previous fact mastered occurs 10% to 20% of the time (three to six problems). The remaining 40% to 50% of the problems on each sheet are those previously learned by the student, except for those pages labeled as tests, which usually present each fact only once.

Each student should complete a timed test every day if possible, starting with the lowest fact on the progress chart for that student. Remind the students to note the fact written in the upper left-hand corner, which indicates the fact on which they are working. Students must complete all the problems on a sheet accurately in one minute before advancing to the next fact. If the student has not completely and accurately answered all the problems when the minute has elapsed, he or she must complete a test for the same fact the next day.

If a student can pass the Zero Rule test, he or she has demonstrated the hand dexterity needed to complete the page in one minute. However, if students have extreme difficulty passing each fact page, you may wish to lengthen the amount of time allowed to complete the page by five or ten seconds.

It is important to allow students to see their progress on the same fact. All attempted tests may be left in the folder and the same fact test added on top for the next day. Students will become more proficient each time they are retested on the same fact until they finally master it.

Not all students will complete the entire program, but they will possess a greater proficiency of the facts they have mastered. Mastery, rather than completion, is the goal of the program.

Dear Parent,

In order to develop a good mathematics foundation, it is important that your child learn basic addition and subtraction facts. The <u>One-Minute Math Developmental Drill</u> program enables children to achieve this goal. The idea behind this program is that children must master a particular math fact before they are introduced to a new fact.

A flash card will be sent home each time your child begins learning a new subtraction fact. The flash cards will help your child memorize these facts more readily. Please have your child practice daily with all of the flash cards you have received. He or she should work toward answering each card in less than two seconds. Help your child with this activity if possible. Since it may take several days to commit some facts to memory, be patient with your child. Children will not learn all facts at the same rate. Do not expect your child to bring home a new flash card every day.

The Level A Subtraction program includes:

1. Pretest and posttest for placement and evaluation

2. 47 individual fact tests on minuends zero to ten

   a. Each test contains 30 problems

   b. The particular fact a student is learning is covered in 40% of the test

   c. The previously learned fact is covered in 10% to 20% of the test

3. 66 flash cards for practicing the selected facts

4. Certificate upon completion

Thank you for working with me on this program.
Please contact me if you have any questions or concerns.

Sincerely,

Reproducible Art

vi

Manipulative Mat

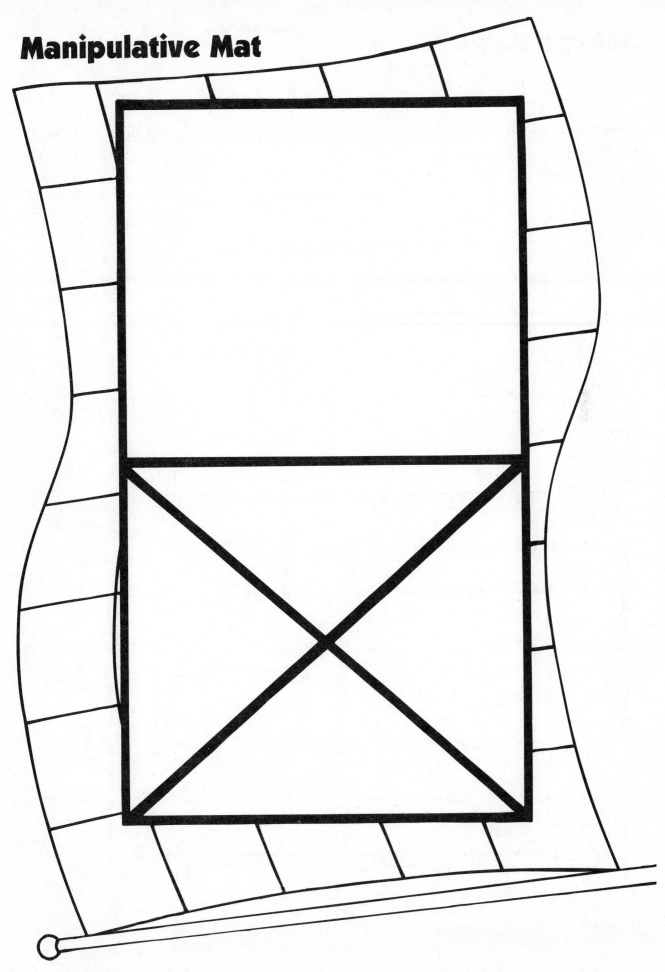

FS-23243 One-Minute Math Level A Subtraction

Activity Page

Name _____

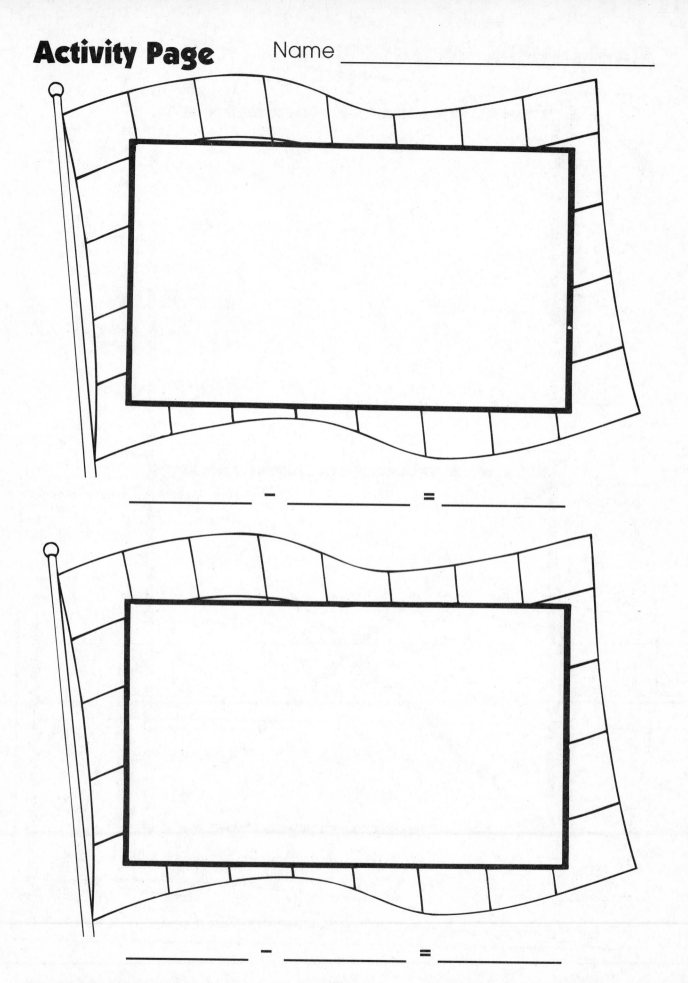

_____ - _____ = _____

_____ - _____ = _____

FS-23243 One-Minute Math Level A Subtraction

Awards and Certificate

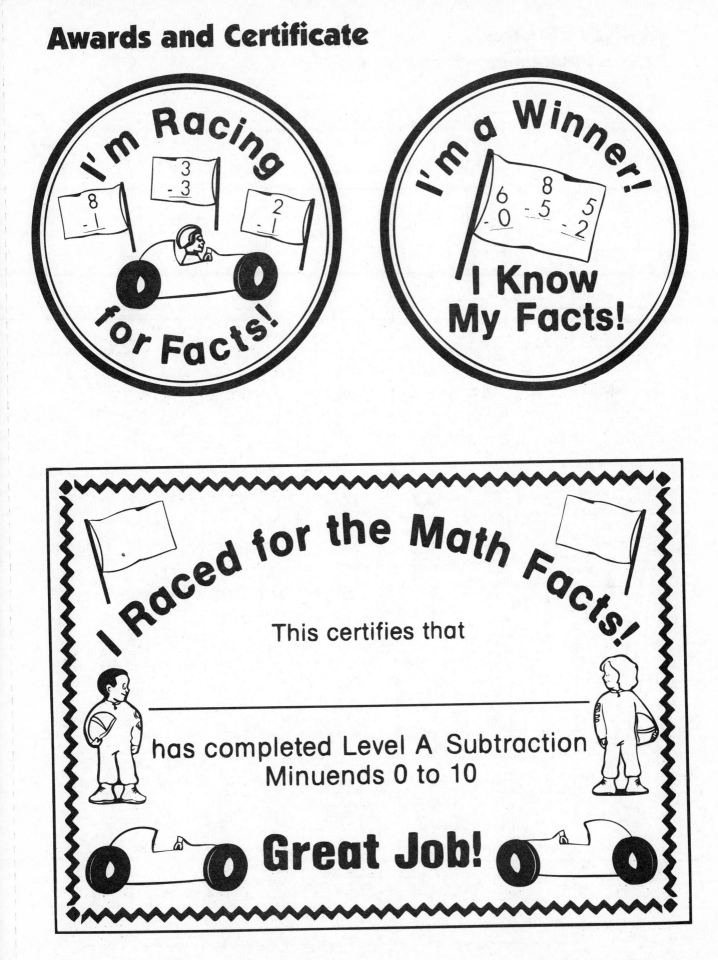

I'm Racing for Facts!

$\frac{8}{-1}$ $\frac{3}{-3}$ $\frac{2}{-1}$

I'm a Winner! I Know My Facts!

$\frac{6}{-0}$ $\frac{8}{-5}$ $\frac{5}{-2}$

I Raced for the Math Facts!

This certifies that

_____

has completed Level A Subtraction
Minuends 0 to 10

Great Job!

FS-23243 One-Minute Math Level A Subtraction

Progress Chart
Level A Subtraction   Minuends 0 to 10

Name	Pre-test	0 Rule	1 Rule	2-2	3-2	4-2	5-2	6-2	7-2	8-2	9-2	10-2	3-3	4-3	5-3	6-3	7-3	8-3	9-3	10-3	4-4	5-4	6-4	7-4	8-4

Progress Chart
Level A Subtraction   Minuends 0 to 10

Name	9 -4	10 -4	5 -5	6 -5	7 -5	8 -5	9 -5	10 -5	6 -6	7 -6	8 -6	9 -6	10 -6	7 -7	8 -7	9 -7	10 -7	8 -8	9 -8	10 -8	9 -9	10 -9	10 -10	Test

xi

Student Progress Chart

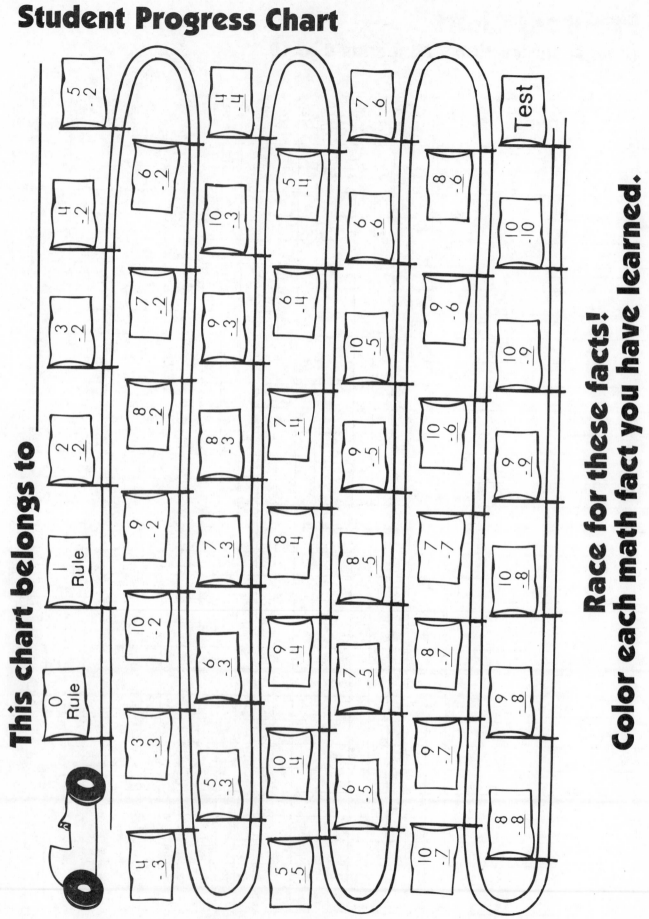

This chart belongs to _____

Race for these facts!
Color each math fact you have learned.

3 − 2	10 − 1	6 − 0	3 − 2	2 − 2
5 − 1	3 − 2	5 − 0	8 − 1	3 − 2
3 − 2	2 − 2	9 − 0	3 − 2	2 − 1
6 − 1	3 − 2	0 − 0	2 − 2	3 − 2
3 − 2	2 − 2	3 − 2	7 − 1	5 − 0
8 − 0	3 − 2	9 − 1	3 − 2	2 − 2

Name _____

$$\begin{array}{r} 4 \\ -\ 2 \\ \hline \end{array} \qquad \begin{array}{r} 3 \\ -\ 1 \\ \hline \end{array} \qquad \begin{array}{r} 2 \\ -\ 2 \\ \hline \end{array} \qquad \begin{array}{r} 4 \\ -\ 2 \\ \hline \end{array} \qquad \begin{array}{r} 3 \\ -\ 2 \\ \hline \end{array}$$

$$\begin{array}{r} 9 \\ -\ 0 \\ \hline \end{array} \qquad \begin{array}{r} 4 \\ -\ 2 \\ \hline \end{array} \qquad \begin{array}{r} 3 \\ -\ 2 \\ \hline \end{array} \qquad \begin{array}{r} 6 \\ -\ 0 \\ \hline \end{array} \qquad \begin{array}{r} 4 \\ -\ 2 \\ \hline \end{array}$$

$$\begin{array}{r} 4 \\ -\ 2 \\ \hline \end{array} \qquad \begin{array}{r} 4 \\ -\ 1 \\ \hline \end{array} \qquad \begin{array}{r} 2 \\ -\ 2 \\ \hline \end{array} \qquad \begin{array}{r} 4 \\ -\ 2 \\ \hline \end{array} \qquad \begin{array}{r} 8 \\ -\ 1 \\ \hline \end{array}$$

$$\begin{array}{r} 9 \\ -\ 1 \\ \hline \end{array} \qquad \begin{array}{r} 4 \\ -\ 2 \\ \hline \end{array} \qquad \begin{array}{r} 10 \\ -\ 0 \\ \hline \end{array} \qquad \begin{array}{r} 3 \\ -\ 2 \\ \hline \end{array} \qquad \begin{array}{r} 4 \\ -\ 2 \\ \hline \end{array}$$

$$\begin{array}{r} 3 \\ -\ 2 \\ \hline \end{array} \qquad \begin{array}{r} 4 \\ -\ 2 \\ \hline \end{array} \qquad \begin{array}{r} 2 \\ -\ 2 \\ \hline \end{array} \qquad \begin{array}{r} 4 \\ -\ 2 \\ \hline \end{array} \qquad \begin{array}{r} 6 \\ -\ 1 \\ \hline \end{array}$$

$$\begin{array}{r} 8 \\ -\ 0 \\ \hline \end{array} \qquad \begin{array}{r} 3 \\ -\ 2 \\ \hline \end{array} \qquad \begin{array}{r} 4 \\ -\ 2 \\ \hline \end{array} \qquad \begin{array}{r} 5 \\ -\ 0 \\ \hline \end{array} \qquad \begin{array}{r} 4 \\ -\ 2 \\ \hline \end{array}$$

$$\begin{array}{r} 3 \\ -\ 2 \\ \hline \end{array} \qquad \begin{array}{r} 5 \\ -\ 2 \\ \hline \end{array} \qquad \begin{array}{r} 2 \\ -\ 0 \\ \hline \end{array} \qquad \begin{array}{r} 5 \\ -\ 2 \\ \hline \end{array} \qquad \begin{array}{r} 4 \\ -\ 2 \\ \hline \end{array}$$

$$\begin{array}{r} 5 \\ -\ 2 \\ \hline \end{array} \qquad \begin{array}{r} 4 \\ -\ 2 \\ \hline \end{array} \qquad \begin{array}{r} 5 \\ -\ 2 \\ \hline \end{array} \qquad \begin{array}{r} 4 \\ -\ 1 \\ \hline \end{array} \qquad \begin{array}{r} 5 \\ -\ 0 \\ \hline \end{array}$$

$$\begin{array}{r} 6 \\ -\ 1 \\ \hline \end{array} \qquad \begin{array}{r} 5 \\ -\ 2 \\ \hline \end{array} \qquad \begin{array}{r} 3 \\ -\ 2 \\ \hline \end{array} \qquad \begin{array}{r} 3 \\ -\ 0 \\ \hline \end{array} \qquad \begin{array}{r} 5 \\ -\ 2 \\ \hline \end{array}$$

$$\begin{array}{r} 5 \\ -\ 2 \\ \hline \end{array} \qquad \begin{array}{r} 3 \\ -\ 1 \\ \hline \end{array} \qquad \begin{array}{r} 4 \\ -\ 2 \\ \hline \end{array} \qquad \begin{array}{r} 5 \\ -\ 2 \\ \hline \end{array} \qquad \begin{array}{r} 4 \\ -\ 0 \\ \hline \end{array}$$

$$\begin{array}{r} 2 \\ -\ 1 \\ \hline \end{array} \qquad \begin{array}{r} 5 \\ -\ 2 \\ \hline \end{array} \qquad \begin{array}{r} 3 \\ -\ 2 \\ \hline \end{array} \qquad \begin{array}{r} 4 \\ -\ 2 \\ \hline \end{array} \qquad \begin{array}{r} 5 \\ -\ 2 \\ \hline \end{array}$$

$$\begin{array}{r} 5 \\ -\ 2 \\ \hline \end{array} \qquad \begin{array}{r} 4 \\ -\ 2 \\ \hline \end{array} \qquad \begin{array}{r} 5 \\ -\ 2 \\ \hline \end{array} \qquad \begin{array}{r} 3 \\ -\ 2 \\ \hline \end{array} \qquad \begin{array}{r} 1 \\ -\ 1 \\ \hline \end{array}$$

5	2	6	10	6
− 2	− 2	− 2	− 1	− 2

6	2	9	6	5
− 2	− 0	− 1	− 2	− 2

5	6	1	2	6
− 2	− 2	− 0	− 2	− 2

6	3	6	8	4
− 2	− 2	− 2	− 1	− 2

0	6	4	6	5
− 0	− 2	− 2	− 2	− 2

3	5	6	7	6
− 2	− 2	− 2	− 1	− 2

7 − 2	3 − 2	6 − 0	7 − 2	5 − 2
2 − 2	7 − 2	2 − 1	6 − 2	7 − 2
7 − 2	6 − 2	7 − 2	9 − 1	3 − 2
3 − 0	7 − 2	5 − 2	7 − 2	6 − 2
6 − 2	4 − 2	7 − 2	7 − 1	7 − 2
7 − 2	5 − 1	6 − 2	7 − 2	4 − 2

8 − 2	1 − 1	7 − 2	6 − 2	8 − 2
5 − 2	8 − 2	6 − 0	8 − 2	3 − 2
7 − 2	9 − 1	8 − 2	6 − 2	8 − 2
8 − 2	2 − 2	7 − 2	8 − 2	4 − 0
4 − 2	8 − 2	2 − 0	7 − 2	8 − 2
8 − 2	8 − 1	8 − 2	5 − 2	7 − 2

10

8 − 2	2 − 2	9 − 2	4 − 1	9 − 2
9 − 2	8 − 2	7 − 0	9 − 2	6 − 1
3 − 2	9 − 2	7 − 2	10 − 0	9 − 2
9 − 2	5 − 2	9 − 2	9 − 1	8 − 2
8 − 2	9 − 2	4 − 2	9 − 2	7 − 2
6 − 2	8 − 2	9 − 2	5 − 2	9 − 2

4 − 2	10 − 2	5 − 1	10 − 2	9 − 2
10 − 2	5 − 2	9 − 2	4 − 0	10 − 2
9 − 2	4 − 1	10 − 2	8 − 2	10 − 2
6 − 2	10 − 2	3 − 2	10 − 2	9 − 2
10 − 2	8 − 2	10 − 2	9 − 2	2 − 0
2 − 2	10 − 2	2 − 1	10 − 2	7 − 2

FS-23243 One-Minute Math Level A Subtraction

Name _____

3 − 1	3 − 3	10 − 2	6 − 2	3 − 3
3 − 3	7 − 2	6 − 0	3 − 3	3 − 2
8 − 2	2 − 2	3 − 3	10 − 2	3 − 3
3 − 3	10 − 2	7 − 1	3 − 3	9 − 2
5 − 2	3 − 3	9 − 0	10 − 2	3 − 3
3 − 3	8 − 1	3 − 3	4 − 2	10 − 2

Name _____

4 − 3	6 − 2	10 − 2	4 − 3	3 − 3
5 − 2	4 − 3	3 − 3	6 − 1	4 − 3
4 − 3	3 − 0	4 − 3	3 − 2	3 − 3
8 − 2	4 − 3	2 − 2	4 − 3	7 − 2
4 − 3	7 − 1	3 − 3	8 − 0	4 − 3
4 − 3	9 − 2	4 − 3	4 − 2	3 − 3

14

3 − 2	5 − 3	10 − 2	4 − 3	5 − 3
5 − 3	2 − 2	4 − 3	5 − 3	5 − 2
4 − 3	6 − 1	5 − 3	8 − 2	5 − 3
5 − 3	4 − 3	3 − 0	5 − 3	3 − 3
6 − 2	5 − 3	7 − 2	9 − 2	5 − 3
5 − 3	4 − 2	5 − 3	8 − 1	4 − 3

$$
\begin{array}{r} 6 \\ -\ 3 \\ \hline \end{array}
\qquad
\begin{array}{r} 5 \\ -\ 2 \\ \hline \end{array}
\qquad
\begin{array}{r} 4 \\ -\ 3 \\ \hline \end{array}
\qquad
\begin{array}{r} 6 \\ -\ 3 \\ \hline \end{array}
\qquad
\begin{array}{r} 5 \\ -\ 3 \\ \hline \end{array}
$$

$$
\begin{array}{r} 5 \\ -\ 3 \\ \hline \end{array}
\qquad
\begin{array}{r} 6 \\ -\ 3 \\ \hline \end{array}
\qquad
\begin{array}{r} 10 \\ -\ 2 \\ \hline \end{array}
\qquad
\begin{array}{r} 6 \\ -\ 2 \\ \hline \end{array}
\qquad
\begin{array}{r} 6 \\ -\ 3 \\ \hline \end{array}
$$

$$
\begin{array}{r} 6 \\ -\ 3 \\ \hline \end{array}
\qquad
\begin{array}{r} 7 \\ -\ 0 \\ \hline \end{array}
\qquad
\begin{array}{r} 3 \\ -\ 3 \\ \hline \end{array}
\qquad
\begin{array}{r} 6 \\ -\ 3 \\ \hline \end{array}
\qquad
\begin{array}{r} 7 \\ -\ 2 \\ \hline \end{array}
$$

$$
\begin{array}{r} 10 \\ -\ 1 \\ \hline \end{array}
\qquad
\begin{array}{r} 5 \\ -\ 3 \\ \hline \end{array}
\qquad
\begin{array}{r} 6 \\ -\ 3 \\ \hline \end{array}
\qquad
\begin{array}{r} 9 \\ -\ 2 \\ \hline \end{array}
\qquad
\begin{array}{r} 6 \\ -\ 3 \\ \hline \end{array}
$$

$$
\begin{array}{r} 4 \\ -\ 2 \\ \hline \end{array}
\qquad
\begin{array}{r} 6 \\ -\ 3 \\ \hline \end{array}
\qquad
\begin{array}{r} 3 \\ -\ 2 \\ \hline \end{array}
\qquad
\begin{array}{r} 6 \\ -\ 3 \\ \hline \end{array}
\qquad
\begin{array}{r} 5 \\ -\ 3 \\ \hline \end{array}
$$

$$
\begin{array}{r} 6 \\ -\ 3 \\ \hline \end{array}
\qquad
\begin{array}{r} 2 \\ -\ 2 \\ \hline \end{array}
\qquad
\begin{array}{r} 6 \\ -\ 3 \\ \hline \end{array}
\qquad
\begin{array}{r} 5 \\ -\ 3 \\ \hline \end{array}
\qquad
\begin{array}{r} 8 \\ -\ 2 \\ \hline \end{array}
$$

7 − 3	2 − 2	6 − 3	9 − 2	7 − 3
10 − 2	7 − 3	8 − 2	7 − 3	3 − 2
6 − 3	5 − 3	7 − 3	6 − 2	7 − 3
7 − 3	6 − 3	5 − 2	7 − 3	4 − 2
3 − 3	7 − 3	6 − 1	6 − 3	7 − 3
7 − 3	7 − 2	7 − 3	4 − 3	6 − 3

8 − 2	8 − 3	6 − 3	8 − 3	7 − 3
8 − 3	10 − 2	7 − 3	4 − 3	8 − 3
3 − 3	8 − 3	4 − 2	8 − 3	9 − 2
7 − 3	6 − 2	8 − 3	3 − 2	8 − 3
8 − 3	5 − 3	7 − 3	8 − 3	7 − 2
5 − 2	8 − 3	2 − 2	7 − 3	8 − 3

Name _____

5	9	10	4	9
− 3	− 3	− 2	− 3	− 3

9	6	8	9	8
− 3	− 2	− 3	− 3	− 2

4	9	9	8	9
− 2	− 3	− 2	− 3	− 3

9	3	9	7	8
− 3	− 3	− 3	− 3	− 3

8	9	3	9	7
− 3	− 3	− 2	− 3	− 2

5	8	9	6	9
− 2	− 3	− 3	− 3	− 3

Name _____

10	5	9	5	10
− 3	− 2	− 3	− 3	− 3

9	10	6	10	7
− 3	− 3	− 2	− 3	− 2

10	8	10	8	10
− 2	− 3	− 3	− 2	− 3

10	6	9	10	9
− 3	− 3	− 3	− 3	− 2

7	10	4	9	10
− 3	− 3	− 2	− 3	− 3

10	4	10	3	9
− 3	− 3	− 3	− 3	− 3

Name _____

10 − 3	4 − 4	9 − 3	7 − 2	4 − 4
4 − 4	5 − 2	10 − 3	4 − 4	6 − 3
5 − 3	4 − 4	6 − 2	9 − 2	4 − 4
4 − 4	7 − 3	4 − 4	4 − 3	10 − 3
10 − 2	4 − 4	10 − 3	4 − 4	8 − 2
4 − 4	8 − 3	3 − 3	10 − 3	4 − 4

4 − 4	7 − 2	5 − 4	10 − 3	5 − 4
5 − 4	8 − 2	7 − 3	5 − 4	5 − 3
3 − 3	5 − 4	9 − 3	4 − 4	5 − 4
5 − 4	10 − 2	5 − 4	6 − 2	4 − 4
4 − 4	5 − 4	9 − 2	5 − 4	8 − 3
6 − 3	4 − 4	5 − 4	4 − 3	5 − 4

Name _____

$$\begin{array}{r} 6 \\ -\ 4 \\ \hline \end{array} \qquad \begin{array}{r} 7 \\ -\ 3 \\ \hline \end{array} \qquad \begin{array}{r} 10 \\ -\ 3 \\ \hline \end{array} \qquad \begin{array}{r} 6 \\ -\ 4 \\ \hline \end{array} \qquad \begin{array}{r} 6 \\ -\ 2 \\ \hline \end{array}$$

$$\begin{array}{r} 8 \\ -\ 2 \\ \hline \end{array} \qquad \begin{array}{r} 6 \\ -\ 4 \\ \hline \end{array} \qquad \begin{array}{r} 6 \\ -\ 3 \\ \hline \end{array} \qquad \begin{array}{r} 5 \\ -\ 4 \\ \hline \end{array} \qquad \begin{array}{r} 6 \\ -\ 4 \\ \hline \end{array}$$

$$\begin{array}{r} 6 \\ -\ 4 \\ \hline \end{array} \qquad \begin{array}{r} 4 \\ -\ 3 \\ \hline \end{array} \qquad \begin{array}{r} 6 \\ -\ 4 \\ \hline \end{array} \qquad \begin{array}{r} 9 \\ -\ 2 \\ \hline \end{array} \qquad \begin{array}{r} 5 \\ -\ 4 \\ \hline \end{array}$$

$$\begin{array}{r} 5 \\ -\ 4 \\ \hline \end{array} \qquad \begin{array}{r} 6 \\ -\ 4 \\ \hline \end{array} \qquad \begin{array}{r} 8 \\ -\ 3 \\ \hline \end{array} \qquad \begin{array}{r} 6 \\ -\ 4 \\ \hline \end{array} \qquad \begin{array}{r} 5 \\ -\ 3 \\ \hline \end{array}$$

$$\begin{array}{r} 9 \\ -\ 3 \\ \hline \end{array} \qquad \begin{array}{r} 5 \\ -\ 4 \\ \hline \end{array} \qquad \begin{array}{r} 6 \\ -\ 4 \\ \hline \end{array} \qquad \begin{array}{r} 7 \\ -\ 2 \\ \hline \end{array} \qquad \begin{array}{r} 6 \\ -\ 4 \\ \hline \end{array}$$

$$\begin{array}{r} 6 \\ -\ 4 \\ \hline \end{array} \qquad \begin{array}{r} 10 \\ -\ 2 \\ \hline \end{array} \qquad \begin{array}{r} 4 \\ -\ 4 \\ \hline \end{array} \qquad \begin{array}{r} 6 \\ -\ 4 \\ \hline \end{array} \qquad \begin{array}{r} 5 \\ -\ 4 \\ \hline \end{array}$$

6 − 4	4 − 3	7 − 4	6 − 3	7 − 4
7 − 4	8 − 3	6 − 1	7 − 4	5 − 3
10 − 3	7 − 4	4 − 2	6 − 4	7 − 4
7 − 4	4 − 4	7 − 4	5 − 2	6 − 4
6 − 4	7 − 4	7 − 3	7 − 4	5 − 4
10 − 2	6 − 4	7 − 4	9 − 3	7 − 4

Name _____

8 − 4	9 − 0	7 − 4	8 − 4	10 − 3
7 − 4	8 − 4	2 − 2	5 − 3	8 − 4
8 − 4	9 − 2	8 − 4	6 − 3	7 − 4
7 − 4	8 − 4	9 − 3	8 − 4	7 − 3
8 − 3	4 − 3	8 − 4	8 − 2	8 − 4
8 − 4	6 − 4	7 − 4	8 − 4	5 − 4

Name _____

8 − 3	9 − 4	7 − 4	9 − 4	10 − 2
9 − 4	7 − 3	8 − 4	9 − 3	9 − 4
9 − 2	9 − 4	6 − 4	9 − 4	8 − 4
8 − 4	10 − 3	9 − 4	4 − 3	9 − 4
9 − 4	8 − 4	5 − 3	9 − 4	5 − 4
6 − 3	9 − 4	4 − 4	8 − 4	9 − 4

Name _____

10 − 4	7 − 3	7 − 4	10 − 4	6 − 3
7 − 2	10 − 4	6 − 2	9 − 4	10 − 4
10 − 4	9 − 4	10 − 4	9 − 3	8 − 4
5 − 4	10 − 4	9 − 4	8 − 3	10 − 4
10 − 4	8 − 2	6 − 4	10 − 4	9 − 4
9 − 4	10 − 4	10 − 3	9 − 2	10 − 4

$$\begin{array}{r} 5 \\ -\ 5 \\ \hline \end{array} \qquad \begin{array}{r} 10 \\ -\ 3 \\ \hline \end{array} \qquad \begin{array}{r} 3 \\ -\ 2 \\ \hline \end{array} \qquad \begin{array}{r} 5 \\ -\ 5 \\ \hline \end{array} \qquad \begin{array}{r} 9 \\ -\ 4 \\ \hline \end{array}$$

$$\begin{array}{r} 10 \\ -\ 2 \\ \hline \end{array} \qquad \begin{array}{r} 5 \\ -\ 5 \\ \hline \end{array} \qquad \begin{array}{r} 9 \\ -\ 3 \\ \hline \end{array} \qquad \begin{array}{r} 10 \\ -\ 4 \\ \hline \end{array} \qquad \begin{array}{r} 5 \\ -\ 5 \\ \hline \end{array}$$

$$\begin{array}{r} 10 \\ -\ 4 \\ \hline \end{array} \qquad \begin{array}{r} 8 \\ -\ 2 \\ \hline \end{array} \qquad \begin{array}{r} 5 \\ -\ 5 \\ \hline \end{array} \qquad \begin{array}{r} 8 \\ -\ 4 \\ \hline \end{array} \qquad \begin{array}{r} 5 \\ -\ 5 \\ \hline \end{array}$$

$$\begin{array}{r} 5 \\ -\ 5 \\ \hline \end{array} \qquad \begin{array}{r} 6 \\ -\ 4 \\ \hline \end{array} \qquad \begin{array}{r} 10 \\ -\ 4 \\ \hline \end{array} \qquad \begin{array}{r} 5 \\ -\ 5 \\ \hline \end{array} \qquad \begin{array}{r} 8 \\ -\ 3 \\ \hline \end{array}$$

$$\begin{array}{r} 5 \\ -\ 4 \\ \hline \end{array} \qquad \begin{array}{r} 5 \\ -\ 5 \\ \hline \end{array} \qquad \begin{array}{r} 7 \\ -\ 3 \\ \hline \end{array} \qquad \begin{array}{r} 10 \\ -\ 4 \\ \hline \end{array} \qquad \begin{array}{r} 5 \\ -\ 5 \\ \hline \end{array}$$

$$\begin{array}{r} 5 \\ -\ 5 \\ \hline \end{array} \qquad \begin{array}{r} 10 \\ -\ 4 \\ \hline \end{array} \qquad \begin{array}{r} 9 \\ -\ 2 \\ \hline \end{array} \qquad \begin{array}{r} 5 \\ -\ 5 \\ \hline \end{array} \qquad \begin{array}{r} 7 \\ -\ 4 \\ \hline \end{array}$$

Name _____

5 − 5	6 − 5	10 − 4	6 − 4	6 − 5
6 − 5	10 − 3	9 − 3	6 − 5	8 − 1
5 − 2	6 − 5	4 − 2	5 − 5	6 − 5
6 − 5	9 − 4	6 − 2	6 − 5	5 − 5
7 − 4	6 − 5	5 − 5	8 − 4	6 − 5
6 − 5	8 − 3	6 − 5	7 − 3	5 − 5

29

$$
\begin{array}{r} 8 \\ -\ 4 \\ \hline \end{array} \qquad
\begin{array}{r} 7 \\ -\ 5 \\ \hline \end{array} \qquad
\begin{array}{r} 8 \\ -\ 2 \\ \hline \end{array} \qquad
\begin{array}{r} 6 \\ -\ 5 \\ \hline \end{array} \qquad
\begin{array}{r} 7 \\ -\ 5 \\ \hline \end{array}
$$

$$
\begin{array}{r} 7 \\ -\ 5 \\ \hline \end{array} \qquad
\begin{array}{r} 6 \\ -\ 3 \\ \hline \end{array} \qquad
\begin{array}{r} 9 \\ -\ 4 \\ \hline \end{array} \qquad
\begin{array}{r} 7 \\ -\ 5 \\ \hline \end{array} \qquad
\begin{array}{r} 7 \\ -\ 2 \\ \hline \end{array}
$$

$$
\begin{array}{r} 6 \\ -\ 5 \\ \hline \end{array} \qquad
\begin{array}{r} 7 \\ -\ 5 \\ \hline \end{array} \qquad
\begin{array}{r} 10 \\ -\ 2 \\ \hline \end{array} \qquad
\begin{array}{r} 7 \\ -\ 4 \\ \hline \end{array} \qquad
\begin{array}{r} 7 \\ -\ 5 \\ \hline \end{array}
$$

$$
\begin{array}{r} 7 \\ -\ 5 \\ \hline \end{array} \qquad
\begin{array}{r} 5 \\ -\ 3 \\ \hline \end{array} \qquad
\begin{array}{r} 7 \\ -\ 5 \\ \hline \end{array} \qquad
\begin{array}{r} 9 \\ -\ 2 \\ \hline \end{array} \qquad
\begin{array}{r} 6 \\ -\ 5 \\ \hline \end{array}
$$

$$
\begin{array}{r} 6 \\ -\ 5 \\ \hline \end{array} \qquad
\begin{array}{r} 7 \\ -\ 5 \\ \hline \end{array} \qquad
\begin{array}{r} 6 \\ -\ 2 \\ \hline \end{array} \qquad
\begin{array}{r} 10 \\ -\ 4 \\ \hline \end{array} \qquad
\begin{array}{r} 7 \\ -\ 5 \\ \hline \end{array}
$$

$$
\begin{array}{r} 7 \\ -\ 5 \\ \hline \end{array} \qquad
\begin{array}{r} 4 \\ -\ 3 \\ \hline \end{array} \qquad
\begin{array}{r} 6 \\ -\ 5 \\ \hline \end{array} \qquad
\begin{array}{r} 7 \\ -\ 5 \\ \hline \end{array} \qquad
\begin{array}{r} 5 \\ -\ 5 \\ \hline \end{array}
$$

         FS-23243 One-Minute Math Level A Subtraction

Name _____

7 − 2	8 − 5	6 − 3	8 − 5	6 − 5
8 − 5	6 − 4	7 − 5	10 − 3	8 − 5
7 − 5	8 − 5	8 − 3	8 − 5	5 − 4
10 − 4	7 − 5	8 − 5	5 − 5	8 − 5
8 − 5	9 − 4	7 − 5	8 − 5	8 − 4
7 − 4	8 − 5	9 − 3	7 − 5	8 − 5

Name _____

10	9	7	5	9
− 3	− 5	− 3	− 4	− 5

9	6	9	9	8
− 5	− 2	− 5	− 3	− 5

4	9	8	8	9
− 3	− 5	− 5	− 3	− 5

9	8	5	9	8
− 5	− 2	− 5	− 5	− 5

8	9	6	7	9
− 5	− 5	− 4	− 5	− 5

9	9	9	6	8
− 5	− 2	− 5	− 5	− 5

7 − 4	10 − 5	9 − 5	10 − 3	10 − 5
10 − 5	9 − 3	6 − 4	10 − 5	9 − 5
9 − 4	10 − 5	8 − 5	9 − 2	10 − 5
10 − 5	7 − 5	9 − 5	10 − 5	5 − 5
9 − 5	10 − 5	8 − 4	10 − 4	10 − 5
10 − 5	6 − 5	10 − 5	10 − 2	9 − 5

Name _____

6 − 6	8 − 4	10 − 5	9 − 3	6 − 6
6 − 5	6 − 6	7 − 4	6 − 6	9 − 5
6 − 6	9 − 4	6 − 6	10 − 5	5 − 4
10 − 5	6 − 6	8 − 5	6 − 6	7 − 3
7 − 5	10 − 4	6 − 6	10 − 5	6 − 6
6 − 6	10 − 5	6 − 4	6 − 6	5 − 5

Name _____

7 − 6	8 − 1	8 − 5	7 − 6	9 − 2
10 − 3	7 − 6	8 − 4	6 − 6	7 − 6
7 − 6	6 − 6	7 − 5	7 − 6	10 − 5
9 − 3	7 − 6	7 − 4	6 − 6	7 − 6
7 − 6	6 − 6	10 − 2	7 − 6	9 − 4
9 − 5	7 − 6	10 − 4	6 − 6	7 − 6

Name _____

$$
\begin{array}{c} 8 \\ -\ 6 \\ \hline \end{array} \qquad
\begin{array}{c} 6 \\ -\ 4 \\ \hline \end{array} \qquad
\begin{array}{c} 7 \\ -\ 6 \\ \hline \end{array} \qquad
\begin{array}{c} 8 \\ -\ 6 \\ \hline \end{array} \qquad
\begin{array}{c} 7 \\ -\ 5 \\ \hline \end{array}
$$

$$
\begin{array}{c} 10 \\ -\ 5 \\ \hline \end{array} \qquad
\begin{array}{c} 8 \\ -\ 6 \\ \hline \end{array} \qquad
\begin{array}{c} 10 \\ -\ 4 \\ \hline \end{array} \qquad
\begin{array}{c} 7 \\ -\ 6 \\ \hline \end{array} \qquad
\begin{array}{c} 8 \\ -\ 6 \\ \hline \end{array}
$$

$$
\begin{array}{c} 8 \\ -\ 6 \\ \hline \end{array} \qquad
\begin{array}{c} 5 \\ -\ 5 \\ \hline \end{array} \qquad
\begin{array}{c} 8 \\ -\ 6 \\ \hline \end{array} \qquad
\begin{array}{c} 7 \\ -\ 4 \\ \hline \end{array} \qquad
\begin{array}{c} 7 \\ -\ 6 \\ \hline \end{array}
$$

$$
\begin{array}{c} 6 \\ -\ 5 \\ \hline \end{array} \qquad
\begin{array}{c} 8 \\ -\ 6 \\ \hline \end{array} \qquad
\begin{array}{c} 7 \\ -\ 3 \\ \hline \end{array} \qquad
\begin{array}{c} 8 \\ -\ 6 \\ \hline \end{array} \qquad
\begin{array}{c} 6 \\ -\ 6 \\ \hline \end{array}
$$

$$
\begin{array}{c} 7 \\ -\ 6 \\ \hline \end{array} \qquad
\begin{array}{c} 8 \\ -\ 5 \\ \hline \end{array} \qquad
\begin{array}{c} 8 \\ -\ 6 \\ \hline \end{array} \qquad
\begin{array}{c} 9 \\ -\ 5 \\ \hline \end{array} \qquad
\begin{array}{c} 8 \\ -\ 6 \\ \hline \end{array}
$$

$$
\begin{array}{c} 8 \\ -\ 6 \\ \hline \end{array} \qquad
\begin{array}{c} 8 \\ -\ 4 \\ \hline \end{array} \qquad
\begin{array}{c} 7 \\ -\ 6 \\ \hline \end{array} \qquad
\begin{array}{c} 8 \\ -\ 6 \\ \hline \end{array} \qquad
\begin{array}{c} 9 \\ -\ 4 \\ \hline \end{array}
$$

FS-23243 One-Minute Math Level A Subtraction

Name _____

9 − 6	8 − 4	7 − 6	9 − 6	9 − 5
8 − 6	7 − 5	9 − 6	10 − 5	9 − 6
6 − 6	9 − 6	8 − 5	9 − 6	8 − 6
9 − 6	9 − 4	9 − 6	7 − 4	8 − 6
8 − 6	9 − 6	10 − 3	9 − 6	10 − 4
7 − 2	8 − 6	9 − 6	6 − 4	9 − 6

10 − 6	8 − 6	7 − 2	10 − 6	9 − 5
6 − 6	10 − 6	9 − 6	7 − 3	10 − 6
10 − 6	9 − 6	7 − 4	10 − 6	7 − 6
8 − 5	10 − 6	6 − 3	9 − 6	10 − 6
10 − 6	8 − 4	10 − 6	10 − 5	9 − 6
9 − 6	10 − 6	6 − 4	10 − 6	7 − 5

Name _____

7 − 7	5 − 4	10 − 6	9 − 5	7 − 7
10 − 6	7 − 7	9 − 4	7 − 7	7 − 6
8 − 5	10 − 6	7 − 7	9 − 6	7 − 7
7 − 7	8 − 6	10 − 5	7 − 7	10 − 6
5 − 3	7 − 7	10 − 6	7 − 5	7 − 7
7 − 7	9 − 3	10 − 4	7 − 7	6 − 2

7 − 7	8 − 7	6 − 6	10 − 6	8 − 7
8 − 7	10 − 4	8 − 7	7 − 5	7 − 7
7 − 6	8 − 7	5 − 4	8 − 7	8 − 5
7 − 7	8 − 6	8 − 7	9 − 6	8 − 7
8 − 7	7 − 3	7 − 7	8 − 7	10 − 5
7 − 7	8 − 7	7 − 2	9 − 5	8 − 7

Name _____

8 − 7	9 − 7	6 − 3	10 − 6	9 − 7
9 − 7	6 − 4	8 − 5	9 − 7	8 − 7
8 − 7	9 − 7	6 − 6	9 − 6	9 − 7
9 − 7	8 − 4	7 − 5	9 − 7	7 − 7
8 − 6	9 − 7	8 − 7	7 − 6	9 − 7
9 − 7	9 − 3	8 − 7	9 − 7	4 − 2

Name _____

8 − 7	10 − 7	10 − 6	7 − 7	10 − 7
10 − 7	7 − 5	10 − 7	9 − 6	9 − 7
8 − 6	10 − 7	9 − 7	10 − 7	9 − 4
10 − 7	8 − 5	10 − 7	7 − 6	9 − 7
9 − 7	10 − 7	9 − 5	10 − 7	8 − 3
9 − 7	8 − 4	10 − 7	10 − 5	10 − 7

9 − 4	8 − 8	8 − 2	10 − 7	8 − 8
8 − 8	10 − 7	8 − 8	10 − 6	7 − 7
8 − 7	8 − 8	9 − 6	8 − 8	9 − 7
8 − 8	7 − 5	10 − 7	8 − 5	8 − 8
10 − 7	8 − 8	7 − 4	8 − 8	8 − 6
8 − 8	7 − 6	8 − 8	10 − 7	5 − 3

Name _____

8 − 8	9 − 8	10 − 7	7 − 4	9 − 8
9 − 8	9 − 6	8 − 5	9 − 8	8 − 7
9 − 5	9 − 8	8 − 8	10 − 5	9 − 8
9 − 8	8 − 8	10 − 6	9 − 8	7 − 7
6 − 6	9 − 8	9 − 7	8 − 8	9 − 8
9 − 8	7 − 6	9 − 8	8 − 6	8 − 8

Name _____

10 − 5	10 − 8	8 − 7	9 − 8	10 − 8
10 − 8	9 − 8	8 − 6	10 − 8	9 − 6
9 − 8	10 − 8	9 − 5	9 − 7	10 − 8
10 − 8	8 − 4	9 − 8	10 − 8	10 − 7
6 − 4	10 − 8	10 − 6	9 − 8	10 − 8
10 − 8	8 − 3	10 − 8	8 − 8	8 − 5

Name _____

8 − 7	9 − 9	9 − 6	10 − 8	9 − 9
9 − 9	10 − 8	7 − 5	9 − 9	10 − 6
6 − 2	9 − 9	10 − 7	10 − 8	9 − 9
9 − 9	10 − 8	6 − 5	9 − 9	9 − 7
10 − 4	9 − 9	8 − 3	10 − 8	9 − 9
9 − 9	9 − 4	9 − 9	10 − 2	9 − 8

FS-23243 One-Minute Math Level A Subtraction

9 − 9	10 − 9	10 − 5	8 − 6	10 − 9
10 − 9	6 − 5	9 − 7	10 − 9	10 − 8
7 − 6	10 − 9	8 − 7	9 − 8	10 − 9
10 − 9	7 − 5	10 − 9	9 − 6	8 − 8
8 − 5	10 − 9	6 − 4	10 − 7	10 − 9
10 − 9	4 − 3	10 − 6	10 − 9	9 − 5

Name _____

10 − 9	10 − 10	9 − 7	10 − 10	10 − 8
10 − 10	8 − 6	10 − 9	8 − 7	10 − 10
9 − 6	10 − 10	9 − 8	10 − 10	10 − 6
10 − 9	10 − 7	10 − 10	10 − 5	10 − 10
10 − 10	9 − 5	10 − 9	10 − 10	8 − 8
9 − 9	10 − 10	8 − 4	10 − 9	10 − 10

7 − 3	10 − 3	9 − 8	9 − 5	10 − 10
8 − 6	10 − 9	9 − 3	7 − 6	10 − 5
8 − 5	9 − 7	7 − 5	8 − 3	10 − 7
6 − 5	10 − 8	8 − 4	10 − 6	9 − 4
7 − 4	10 − 4	8 − 1	9 − 6	3 − 0
5 − 4	9 − 2	8 − 7	6 − 4	10 − 2

Answer Key
Level A Subtraction

Page one   Pretest

2	1	8	1	7
2	4	4	1	5
6	1	5	2	1
3	7	3	6	3
7	4	4	0	1
5	2	3	3	2

Page two   (0-Rule)

4	6	8	3	2
5	0	1	9	3
10	2	4	6	7
8	10	1	9	3
0	8	5	4	2
7	6	9	2	1

Page three   (1-Rule)

9	4	0	5	3
3	2	6	6	2
5	1	4	8	8
8	3	9	5	7
8	1	0	7	9
7	7	10	6	9

Page four   (2-2)

0	9	9	0	1
4	0	2	3	0
0	5	0	4	7
10	0	4	0	8
0	3	6	6	0
7	0	8	0	0

Page five   (3-2)

1	9	6	1	0
4	1	5	7	1
1	0	9	1	1
5	1	0	0	1
1	0	1	6	5
8	1	8	1	0

Page six   (4-2)

2	2	0	2	1
9	2	1	6	2
2	3	0	2	7
8	2	10	1	2
1	2	0	2	5
8	1	2	5	2

Page seven   (5-2)

1	3	2	3	2
3	2	3	3	5
5	3	1	3	3
3	2	2	3	4
1	3	1	2	3
3	2	3	1	0

Page eight   (6-2)

3	0	4	9	4
4	2	8	4	3
3	4	1	0	4
4	1	4	7	2
0	4	2	4	3
1	3	4	6	4

Page nine   (7-2)

5	1	6	5	3
0	5	1	4	5
5	4	5	8	1
3	5	3	5	4
4	2	5	6	5
5	4	4	5	2

Page ten   (8-2)

6	0	5	4	6
3	6	6	6	1
5	8	6	4	6
6	0	5	6	4
2	6	2	5	6
6	7	6	3	5

Page eleven   (9-2)

6	0	7	3	7
7	6	7	7	5
1	7	5	10	7
7	3	7	8	6
6	7	2	7	5
4	6	7	3	7

Page twelve   (10-2)

2	8	4	8	7
8	3	7	4	8
7	3	8	6	8
4	8	1	8	7
8	6	8	7	2
0	8	1	8	5

Page thirteen   (3-3)

2	0	8	4	0
0	5	6	0	1
6	0	0	8	0
0	8	6	0	7
3	0	9	8	0
0	7	0	2	8

Page fourteen   (4-3)

1	4	8	1	0
3	1	0	5	1
1	3	1	1	0
6	1	0	1	5
1	6	0	8	1
1	7	1	2	0

Page fifteen   (5-3)

1	2	8	1	2
2	0	1	2	3
1	5	2	6	2
2	1	3	2	0
4	2	5	7	2
2	2	2	7	1

Answer Key
Level A Subtraction

Page sixteen (6-3)

3	3	1	3	2
2	3	8	4	3
3	7	0	3	5
9	2	3	7	3
2	3	1	3	2
3	0	3	2	6

Page seventeen (7-3)

4	0	3	7	4
8	4	6	4	1
3	2	4	4	4
4	3	3	4	2
0	4	5	3	4
4	5	4	1	3

Page eighteen (8-3)

6	5	3	5	4
5	8	4	1	5
0	5	2	5	7
4	4	5	1	5
5	2	4	5	5
3	5	0	4	5

Page nineteen (9-3)

2	6	8	1	6
6	4	5	6	6
2	6	7	5	6
6	0	6	4	5
5	6	1	6	5
3	5	6	3	6

Page twenty (10-3)

7	3	6	2	7
6	7	4	7	5
8	5	7	6	7
7	3	6	7	7
4	7	2	6	7
7	1	7	0	6

Page twenty-one (4-4)

7	0	6	5	0
0	3	7	0	3
2	0	4	7	0
0	4	0	1	7
8	0	7	0	6
0	5	0	7	0

Page twenty-two (5-4)

0	5	1	7	1
1	6	4	1	2
0	1	6	0	1
1	8	1	4	0
0	1	7	1	5
3	0	1	1	1

Page twenty-three (6-4)

2	4	7	2	4
6	2	3	1	2
2	1	2	7	1
1	2	5	2	2
6	1	2	5	2
2	8	0	2	1

Page twenty-four (7-4)

2	1	3	3	3
3	5	5	3	2
7	3	2	2	3
3	0	3	3	2
2	3	4	3	1
8	2	3	6	3

Page twenty-five (8-4)

4	9	3	4	7
3	4	0	2	4
4	7	4	3	3
3	4	6	4	4
5	1	4	6	4
4	2	3	4	1

Page twenty-six (9-4)

5	5	3	5	8
5	4	4	6	5
7	5	2	5	4
4	7	5	1	5
5	4	2	5	1
3	5	0	4	5

Page twenty-seven (10-4)

6	4	3	6	3
5	6	4	5	6
6	5	6	6	4
1	6	5	5	6
6	6	2	6	5
5	6	7	7	6

Page twenty-eight (5-5)

0	7	1	0	5
8	0	6	6	0
6	6	0	4	0
0	2	6	0	5
1	0	4	6	0
0	6	7	0	3

Page twenty-nine (6-5)

0	1	6	2	1
1	7	6	1	7
3	1	2	0	1
1	5	4	1	0
3	1	0	4	1
1	5	1	4	0

Page thirty (7-5)

4	2	6	1	2
2	3	5	2	5
1	2	8	3	2
2	2	2	7	1
1	2	4	6	2
2	1	1	2	0

Answer Key
Level A Subtraction

Page thirty-one (8-5)

5	3	3	3	1
3	2	2	7	3
2	3	5	3	1
6	2	3	0	3
3	5	2	3	4
3	3	6	2	3

Page thirty-six (8-6)

2	2	1	2	2
5	2	6	1	2
2	0	2	3	1
1	2	4	2	0
1	3	2	4	2
2	4	1	2	5

Page forty-one (9-7)

1	2	3	4	2
2	2	3	2	1
1	2	0	3	2
2	4	2	2	0
2	2	1	1	2
2	6	1	2	2

Page thirty-two (9-5)

7	4	4	1	4
4	4	4	6	3
1	4	3	5	4
4	6	0	4	3
3	4	2	2	4
4	7	4	1	3

Page thirty-seven (9-6)

3	4	1	3	4
2	2	3	5	3
0	3	3	3	2
3	5	3	3	2
2	3	7	3	6
5	2	3	2	3

Page forty-two (10-7)

1	3	4	0	3
3	2	3	3	2
2	3	2	3	5
3	3	3	1	2
2	3	4	3	5
2	4	3	5	3

Page thirty-three (10-5)

3	5	4	7	5
5	6	2	5	4
5	5	3	7	5
5	2	4	5	0
4	5	4	6	5
5	1	5	8	4

Page thirty-eight (10-6)

4	2	5	4	4
0	4	3	4	4
4	3	3	4	1
3	4	3	3	4
4	4	4	5	3
3	4	2	4	2

Page forty-three (8-8)

5	0	6	3	0
0	3	0	4	0
1	0	3	0	2
0	2	3	3	0
3	0	3	0	2
0	1	0	3	2

Page thirty-four (6-6)

0	4	5	6	0
1	0	3	0	4
0	5	0	5	1
5	0	3	0	4
2	6	0	5	0
0	5	2	0	0

Page thirty-nine (7-7)

0	1	4	4	0
4	0	5	0	1
3	4	0	3	0
0	2	5	0	4
2	0	4	2	0
0	6	6	0	4

Page forty-four (9-8)

0	1	3	3	1
1	3	3	1	1
4	1	0	5	1
1	0	4	1	0
0	1	2	0	1
1	1	1	2	0

Page thirty-five (7-6)

1	7	3	1	7
7	1	4	0	1
1	0	2	1	5
6	1	3	0	1
1	0	8	1	5
4	1	6	0	1

Page forty (8-7)

0	1	0	4	1
1	6	1	2	0
1	1	1	1	3
0	2	1	3	1
1	4	0	1	5
0	1	5	4	1

Page forty-five (10-8)

5	2	1	1	2
2	1	2	2	3
1	2	4	2	2
2	4	1	2	3
2	2	4	1	2
2	5	2	0	3

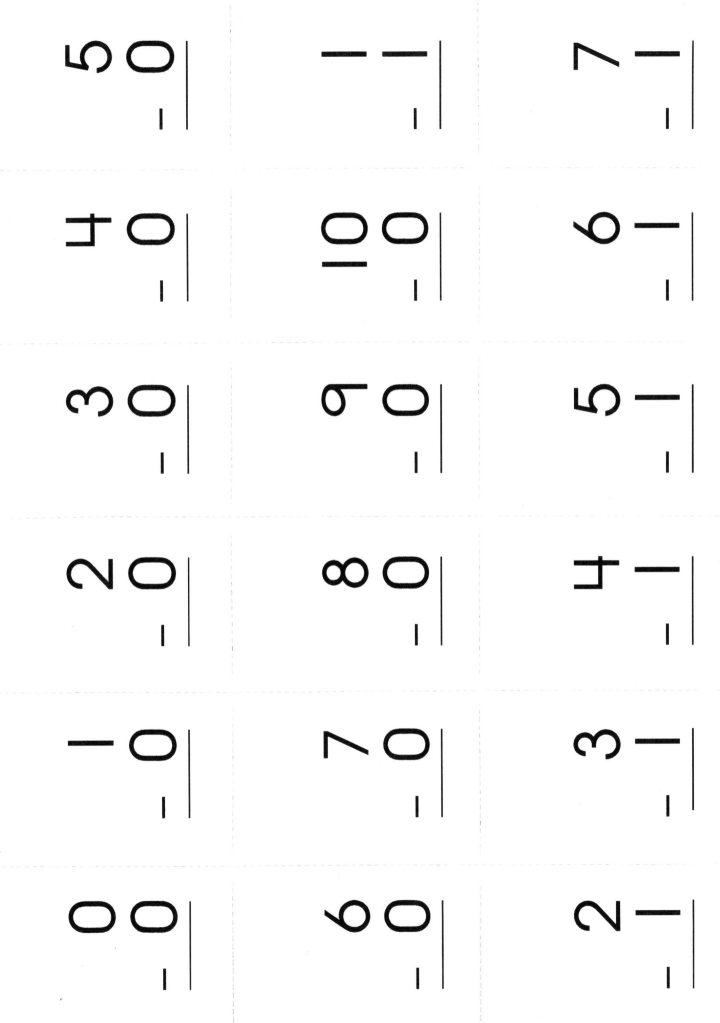

5 − 0	1 − 1	7 − 1
4 − 0	10 − 0	6 − 1
3 − 0	9 − 0	5 − 1
2 − 0	8 − 0	4 − 1
1 − 0	7 − 0	3 − 1
0 − 0	6 − 0	2 − 1

6

0

5

5

10

4

4

9

3

3

8

2

2

7

1

1

6

0

$$4 - 2$$

$$3 - 2$$

$$2 - 2$$

$$10 - 1$$

$$9 - 1$$

$$8 - 1$$

$$10 - 2$$

$$9 - 2$$

$$8 - 2$$

$$7 - 2$$

$$6 - 2$$

$$5 - 2$$

$$8 - 3$$

$$7 - 3$$

$$6 - 3$$

$$5 - 3$$

$$4 - 3$$

$$3 - 3$$

5

8

2

4

7

1

3

6

0

2

5

9

1

4

8

0

3

7

2

2

3

1

1

2

0

0

1

5

6

0

4

5

7

3

4

6

10 − 7	10 − 10	−
9 − 7	10 − 9	−
8 − 7	9 − 9	−
7 − 7	10 − 8	−
10 − 6	9 − 8	−
9 − 6	8 − 8	−

0

3

1

2

0

1

2

0

1

4

0

3